MW01399571

INNER PEACE

Through turbulent times

Hopefully this book is a gift to you. If so, both the author and the person who gave it to you trust it will be an encouragement and a blessing.

Cover design: Sol Graciela Vloebergh
Interior drawings: Michael Branson
ISBN: 9798713063719

Index

We all know what it's like to wake up during the night because something is bugging us, and not be able to get back to sleep. I'm not referring to a physical disturbance, but a mental one. It could be a problem, a conflict, a doubt, or some bad memory that just won't leave us alone. This insomnia may be with us for hours and force upon us a sleepless night. If the matter is serious, we may struggle with it for days, weeks, or even months, to the point where it negatively affects our health.

In this book I would like to share the story of one who many years ago found himself in a situation like the one I just described. He was uneasy, anxious, and unable to sleep. Fortunately he eventually found clear and solid answers to his queries. His story is from centuries past, but it is still extremely relevant, because the doubts and uncertainties that plagued his heart were the same that we experience in our modern day.

I hope his example will help the reader find that sweet and true peace we all want and need, the peace that will bring a life of complete satisfaction and purpose.

Andy Bonikowsky
March, 2021

Nicodemus

Something like this happened to a man named Nicodemus who lived in Jerusalem many years. He was a religious leader, highly respected throughout the nation, both rich and powerful. On the outside, it appeared that he had everything a person could want. But inside he was restless, with a heart full of questions. Even though the general public might have thought he had all the answers, in reality his mind was loaded with uncertainty. Among the questions were those every other thinking person had, the questions of the soul, about the meaning of life, our destiny, and eternity.

This is probably why he developed an interest in a certain mysterious gentleman, one who was causing quite a stir around the country. This man was simple and poor, without a formal education, with few resources, and from a low income family. But he was an itinerant teacher, who taught with such authority in transcendent matters, that multitudes would gather to listen, even to the point of depriving themselves of regular meals. And not only were his lectures profound and thought provoking, but they were accompanied with amazing miracles that could not be discredited. There was no way he could falsify those acts. He had an extraordinary, supernatural power, and Nicodemus was very interested in getting to know him. The man's name was Jesus, and he was from the northern town called Nazareth.

However, Nicodemus had a dilema. Even though he was sure this Nazarene preacher was noble and sincere, his own religious friends and fellow workers hated Jesus with a passion and were actually scheming of ways to silence him. His teachings on ethics and morality heavily contradicted theirs and revealed their vain and proud lifestyle for what it was. They couldn't stand him!

So Nicodemus made the risky decision to pay him a secret visit one night, waiting until dark so as not to be seen by anyone.

The Original Document

But before we continue with the religious teacher and his secret mission, it's important to clear up something about him. He lived about 2,000 years ago, which is a long time. All of the information we have of him is from one source. So it is reasonable to ask the question, How can we know that he was a real person, that he actually lived and isn't just a legend or tale?

The query is a good one that deserves attention, and the answer is both simple and sound. It is founded on the original manuscript that tells his story, which was produced by a man of unquestionable moral integrity. The document is called The Gospel of John and was written around the year 85, by a Jewish fisherman from the Sea of Galilee, also known as the Apostle John. The witnesses and evidence in the decades following its publication leave no room for doubt. The Gospel written by John was an accurate, precise record of the events and the people who knew the Lord Jesus during His life in Israel. Among these would have been the well known pharisee, Nicodemus.

At the back of this book you will find the portions of that original text that have to do with him, and I encourage you take the time to read them.

The Night Time Visit

So let's get back to Nicodemus and his evening plan.

Although the author does not specifically say why he went at night, the context strongly hints that it was because of fear and embarrassment. He had many questions, but to be seen publicly searching for answers from Jesus was unthinkable for someone of his position. However, the doubts in his heart weighed on him so much that finally he decided that making the visit was absolutely necessary. In those days, streets were probably not very well lit at night, so he went then to where Jesus was without being seen.

Nicodemus' opening words to Jesus were that he was sure of his being sent from God. The signs and miracles that He did were unquestionably real and more than enough proof that he was not a charlatan or a cheat.

But the response he got left him confused. "Verily, verily I say unto thee, Except a man be born again, he cannot see the kingdom of God."

Nicodemus would have thought, "Born again? What was that?" He had never heard that phrase before and had no idea what it meant. And what is this about not being able to see the kingdom of God? How could it be that he, one of the most well known and respected religious authorities in the nation, might not even be able to see God without taking this mysterious step?

Nicodemus then followed up with the logical question. How can a man be born if he is old? Can he go back into the womb? That sure sounded absurd.

So Jesus explained: The new birth was not so much being reborn as being born in a different way. Every human being starts their life on earth through the physical birth from his mother. But even when a baby is born he has in him a sinful nature, inherited by all descendants of Adam and Eve. The presence of that sin means that part of their being is dead, or to say it a different way, is separated from God. That dead part is the spirit, the one part that is eternal. This plague of sin condemns each person to a horrible destiny, a spiritual existence forever separated from the Creator. Death is not ceasing to exist; it is being away from God.

Jesus then reminded him of a story from his ancestors, one that as an expert in the Law, Nicodemus would be very familiar with. It was the famous scene in the Sinai desert where

God commanded Moses to raise up a bronze serpent on a pole as a remedy for an infestation of venomous snakes. The children of Israel had sinned against God, and He had sent the snakes as a deadly judgment. However, in His mercy, God also provided a plan for their healing, though it came with a condition. After they were bitten, they were to look up at the brass snake. It was a step of faith, a simple decision that each individual had to make. It made no difference how old they were, what gender they were, or what they had done. Every person who lifted his eyes towards the image of the reptile was cured.

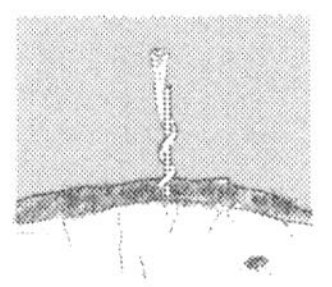

The Raised Snake

Having placed this mental picture in Nicodemus' mind, the Lord surprised him again, with a very odd promise: Just like Moses lifted up the serpent on that pole, one day Jesus would be lifted to provide forgiveness and eternal salvation to anyone who looked to Him for it. His exact words were, "And as Moses lifted up the serpent in the wilderness, even so must the Son of man (a title Jesus had for himself) be lifted up:"

Could Nicodemus possibly have understood this statement? I doubt it very much. In what way could Jesus be compared to the bronze serpent? Why would he be lifted on a pole? How would he stay on it? And what was this about receiving eternal life by looking at Jesus? These were very mysterious words that probably made no sense to the questioning Rabi.

At any rate, the conversation ended there, or at least, what we know of it. In the book of John we hear nothing more about Nicodemus for quite a while, and for all we know, they never met again. Maybe the teacher of Israel returned home with more questions than he had come with, but one thing is certain. He was deeply affected by the meeting. He would never forget the words he had heard, nor the kindness of the Master in receiving him.

A Surprising Defense

In the following months Jesus' fame grew rapidly, especially since the miracles He did were not only before individuals or small groups. Sometimes there were thousands of people listening to him and every family with sick or physically impaired members brought them for healing. On one occasion he turned a few pieces of bread and small fish into enough food to feed 5,000 men and whatever family members they had brought. Meanwhile, the religious groups, led by the Pharisees, were sick of him, and were making plans to arrest and destroy him once and for all.

So one day, according to the seventh chapter in John, they sent some officers to nab him. But when these men arrived at the site where he was teaching, they could not help but hear some of what he was saying. And they were astonished. What beautiful words, and how powerfully he spoke! They had never heard a rabbi or scribe speak that way. His illustrations were so simple and easy to understand. His interpretations of the Old Testament writings were fresh and insightful. His promises were mysterious and inspiring. In the end, the officers were so touched that they returned to the religious leaders without him.

Of course the Pharisees were furious. With heavy sarcasm they asked if the men knew of any from their own group of experts of the Law who had been tricked by the man's teaching. They even insulted the common people for allowing themselves to be duped so easily.

But what a surprise they got when a voice spoke from their own crowd: "Is it normal for us to judge a man before we hear him and know what he's doing?"

It was Nicodemus!

So it is obvious, that after his visit with Jesus that night, Nicodemus had continued thinking about him and going over the surprising ideas he had heard. It is probable that he listened with interest for any commentary or news about him and maybe even tried discreetly to get information about his activities. And all along, there were those doubts and questions about his identity. Could he really be who he claimed to be? Was he truly the Son of God?

Whatever the case, his fellow Pharisees were not about to change their minds. They cared less if what Jesus said was true or not.

They had already decided that he was a fraud, or at least a danger to them, and they were not going to be dissuaded from their goal of eliminating him. This second scene with Nicodemus ends suddenly with an abrupt, "every man went unto his own house."

From this time forward, John the writer, drops any comment about Nicodemus and focuses in on Jesus' ministry. The following chapters include the rescue by Jesus of an adulterous woman, some lectures on the light of the world and the truth, several parables, the resurrection of a man named Lazarus, a number of miraculous healings, some prophecies of his own upcoming death and resurrection, and finally some personal teaching for his disciples.

Jesus also Raised Up

Towards the end of the book, the Pharisees are making headways towards their goal. John describes Jesus' arrest and how various false accusations were leveled against him. The disciples abandon him almost completely, and then, after an interrogation by Pilate the governor, the Christ is crucified. Interestingly, throughout the unusual process of illegal trials and treatment, dozens of precise prophecies are being fulfilled. These prophetical details given in the Old Testament were specifically given for that reason, to identify the

Messiah. By what Jesus did and what was done to him, these were fulfilled perfectly in a way that left no doubt as to his identity.

After they tortured him and nailed him up on the cross, Jesus exclaimed, "It is finished." He then gave up his spirit and died. Right after this a rich man named Joseph of Arimathea approached Pilate. This Joseph was a secret disciple of the Lord, secret because although many of the common people followed the Lord and enjoyed his teaching, it was well known that the powerful ones of Israel were against him. Being sympathetic with Jesus, or showing any interest in him, would not be a smart thing to do for those who lived in affluent circles. However, this wealthy man overcame his fear and asked the governor for Jesus' body. When his request was granted, he went for the body, and was about to move it to his own personal burial place, when another man joined him.

NICODEMUS!

Going Public

Yes! The one who had visited Jesus by night many months earlier, the one who had defended his presumption of innocence among the Pharisees, now showed up to help Joseph. He even brought an expensive mixture of spices to use for wrapping the body.

What had happened? Why was he all of sudden making such a public statement?

Without a doubt it was because he had seen Jesus up on that cross.

That was exactly what the Lord had told him in that unforgettable late night conversation. "As Moses lifted up the serpent in the wilderness, even so must the Son of man be lifted up."

That had to be the determining factor. It was a detail too obvious to ignore, and for Nicodemus, it was the final evidence that wiped out any remaining doubts. Though many Messianic prophecies had been fulfilled in the last few days, for Nicodemus, this one was very special. Jesus had personally told him that it would happen, knowing that when Nicodemus saw it, everything would be perfectly clear.

When it happened, the horrible fear he had had of severe personal consequences from his religious partners vanished like mist in the sun. The life and words of the crucified one were true and what his heart had sensed that first night was true as well: Jesus was the Son of God, God in human flesh, the Messiah of Israel, the eternal Lord, the Savior of the world.

Then Peace Came

A wonderful peace, deep and sweet, flooded his soul, and he immediately went into action. To carry that dead body was too much for one man, and besides, they needed to be extra careful with it. And so it was that Nicodemus showed up with the mixture of spices, to lend Joseph a hand, and the two of them entered together into a glorious and eternal story.

There is nothing quite like enjoying that precious internal peace, especially after years of suffering the torment of fear and the pounding of doubts. Maybe you know what it is like to be afraid, to be continually asking yourself about what is truly important in life. Perhaps you too have had sleepless nights, when certain questions would not leave you alone: Where do I come from? Why am I here? Where am I going?

Well this trio of questions is the most important one we humans will ever consider. How important to not ignore them or shove them aside with cheap distractions! To have doubts is not fun, of course, but they can be healthy and needful. If they take away our sleep, it is because God in his love has sent them to us. He wants to wake us up to the truth that we need him, that in ourselves we do not have real solutions.

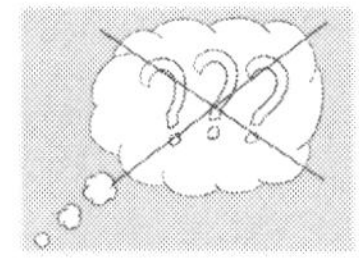

Questions Answered

Nicodemus' story shows us the solution and way to that peace we want so much. His doubts disolved in the reality of who Jesus was. Our deepest questions also find their answers in the Son of God.

Where do I come from? Many say we come from monkeys, or some slime, or an explosion. But our fine human mind has a really hard time accepting that so much incredible design has no designer. Like Nicodemus, we must understand that Jesus himself is our origin. He was who he said he was, and is the Son of God,

Creator of the universe, and all that exists in it. He made us and knows us perfectly.

Why am I here? I exist for Jesus. It makes no sense that we are surrounded by a myriad of things that have obvious purpose, and we who are such awesome beings, are accidents or random chance. We exist for his glory. We are creatures made in his image, made to enjoy fellowship with him forever.

Where am I going? I am going to Jesus. It is illogical that death ends everything. Death does do away with our physical bodies, but it is not the end of us, who think and reason and know we exist. God says that every human being will stand before him in the last day. Those who have searched for him and loved him will live with him for all of eternity. Those who have had no interest in him, who have lived their lives as they pleased and for their own pleasures, will get their wish. They will be separated from him eternally.

It is sad that many people allow themselves to be distracted by a thousand lesser things in order to not think of the more important ones. But sometimes, during the night, even that isn't possible. Like mental tornados, scary and unsettling thoughts swirl around in the heart and rest refuses to come.

Please do not go down that path any more. Follow Nicodemus' example, the one who, realizing he was empty, swallowed his pride, and went looking for answers.

It is a wonderful thing that God has given you the opportunity to know about His Son, to understand the purpose of the cross, where Jesus gave His precious blood for the forgiveness of your sins. He died for you and me. He paid the eternal price of our sin on that horrible tree.

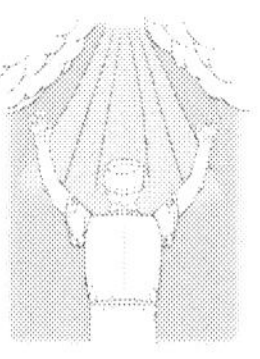

The Wonderful Trio

Once you know that your sins have been forgiven and that Jesus Christ is your Savior, the immediate result will be peace, hope, and joy. Peace, because the doubts and questions will be cleared up by the light of the Gospel. Hope, because the terror of a dark and terrible future will be replaced with the promise of eternal life through the blood of Jesus. And joy, because that peace and hope that spring up in your soul will completely transform your perspective on life. The reasons for anguish and sadness of heart will vanish, and in their place happiness will surge and take over.

This is the amazing truth that millions of people through the centuries have embraced: They first faced their fears and doubts honestly, and then followed the example of the Pharisee who visited Jesus on that night so long ago.

The following prayer is only a sample. The essential thing is that you pray to God from your heart, asking forgiveness and trusting his death on the cross in your place. Writing down your name and date is only a suggestion. If you have any questions, please don't hesitate to write us through the website. God bless you.

Andy Bonikowsky
www.innerpeacebook.org

Dear Lord Jesus, I come to you because I know I need you. I have sinned against you and ask for your forgiveness. Please wash me with the blood you shed on that horrible cross. I trust you for the gift of eternal life. Help me walk with you and learn to love you. Thank you for answering the deepest questions of my heart and replacing my doubts with hope. I look forward to the day when you fulfill your promise to come again for all of us who have put our faith in you.

____

(Name & date)

Hello!

If you have read this far and have been blessed by the book, please share it with someone else who might also be able to benefit from it. If you are not able to pass on your copy, you can order them sent directly from Amazon at a very cheap price. Below are two QR codes. One is to the Amazon page for purchasing and the other is to the INNER PEACE website, where you can also read the book for free.

Andy

INNER PEACE on Amazon

www.innerpeacebook.org

The Gospel of John

Chapter 3:1-21

1. There was a man of the Pharisees, named Nicodemus,
a ruler of the Jews:
2 The same came to Jesus by night, and said unto him,
Rabbi, we know that thou art a teacher come from God:
for no man can do these miracles that thou doest,
except God be with him.
3 Jesus answered and said unto him, Verily, verily, I
say unto thee, Except a man be born again, he cannot
see the kingdom of God.
4 Nicodemus saith unto him, How can a man be born
when he is old? can he enter the second time into his
mother's womb, and be born?
5 Jesus answered, Verily, verily, I say unto thee,
Except a man be born of water and of the Spirit, he
cannot enter into the kingdom of God.
6 That which is born of the flesh is flesh; and that
which is born of the Spirit is spirit.
7 Marvel not that I said unto thee, Ye must be born
again.
8 The wind bloweth where it listeth, and thou hearest the
sound thereof, but canst not tell whence it cometh, and
whither it goeth: so is every one that is born of the Spirit.
9 Nicodemus answered and said unto him, How can
these things be?
10 Jesus answered and said unto him, Art thou a
master of Israel, and knowest not these things?

11 Verily, verily, I say unto thee, We speak that we do
know, and testify that we have seen; and ye receive
not our witness.
12 If I have told you earthly things, and ye believe not,
how shall ye believe, if I tell you of heavenly things?
13 And no man hath ascended up to heaven, but he that
came down from heaven, even the Son of man which is
in heaven.
14 And as Moses lifted up the serpent in the
wilderness, even so must the Son of man be lifted up:
15 That whosoever believeth in him should not perish,
but have eternal life.
16 For God so loved the world, that he gave his only
begotten Son, that whosoever believeth in him should
not perish, but have everlasting life.
17 For God sent not his Son into the world to condemn
the world; but that the world through him might be saved.
18 He that believeth on him is not condemned: but he that
believeth not is condemned already, because he hath not
believed in the name of the only begotten Son of God.
19 And this is the condemnation, that light is come into
the world, and men loved darkness rather than light,
because their deeds were evil.
20 For every one that doeth evil hateth the light,
neither cometh to the light, lest his deeds should be
reproved.
21 But he that doeth truth cometh to the light, that his
deeds may be made manifest, that they are wrought in
God.

Chapter 7:45-52

45 Then came the officers to the chief priests and
Pharisees; and they said unto them, Why have ye not
brought him?
46 The officers answered, Never man spake like this
man.
47 Then answered them the Pharisees, Are ye also
deceived?
48 Have any of the rulers or of the Pharisees believed
on him?
49 But this people who knoweth not the law are
cursed.
50 Nicodemus saith unto them, (he that came to Jesus
by night, being one of them,)
51 Doth our law judge any man, before it hear him, and
know what he doeth?
52 They answered and said unto him, Art thou also of
Galilee? Search, and look: for out of Galilee ariseth no
prophet.
53 And every man went unto his own house.

Chapter 19:38-42

38 And after this Joseph of Arimathaea, being a
disciple of Jesus, but secretly for fear of the Jews,
besought Pilate that he might take away the body of
Jesus: and Pilate gave him leave. He came therefore,
and took the body of Jesus.
39 And there came also Nicodemus, which at the first
came to Jesus by night, and brought a mixture of myrrh
and aloes, about an hundred pound weight.
40 Then took they the body of Jesus, and wound it in
linen clothes with the spices, as the manner of the Jews
is to bury.
41 Now in the place where he was crucified there was a
garden; and in the garden a new sepulchre, wherein was
never man yet laid.
42 There laid they Jesus therefore because of the
Jews' preparation day; for the sepulchre was nigh at
hand.

For what shall it profit a man, if he shall gain
the whole world, and lose his own soul?
(Jesus)

Made in the USA
Columbia, SC
16 November 2024

46721959R00026